GEO

8|04

P9-EEC-529

CIRCULATING WITH THE LISTED PROBLEM(S):

Lexile: _____

AR/BL: _____ 1.0 _____

AR Points: _____ 0.5 _____

Cats on the Farm

by Mari C. Schuh

Consulting Editor: Gail Saunders-Smith, Ph.D.

Consultant: Cary J. Trexler, Ph.D., Assistant Professor
California Agricultural Experiment Station
University of California, Davis

Pebble Books

an imprint of Capstone Press
Mankato, Minnesota

Pebble Books are published by Capstone Press
151 Good Counsel Drive, P.O. Box 669, Mankato, Minnesota 56002
http://www.capstonepress.com

1 2 3 4 5 6 08 07 06 05 04 03

Library of Congress Cataloging-in-Publication Data
Schuh, Mari C., 1975–
    Cats on the farm / by Mari C. Schuh.
    p. cm.—(On the farm)
    Summary: Photographs and simple text describe cats and the lives they live
on the farm.
    Includes bibliographical references and index.
    ISBN 0-7368-3422-2 (softcover) ISBN 0-7368-1660-7 (hardcover)
    1. Cats—Juvenile literature. [1. Cats.] I. Title. II. Series: Schuh, Mari C., 1975– .
On the farm.
SF445.7.S355 2003
636.8—dc21   2002009485

Note to Parents and Teachers

The On the Farm series supports national science standards related to life science. This book describes and illustrates cats and their lives on the farm. The photographs support early readers in understanding the text. The repetition of words and phrases helps early readers learn new words. This book also introduces early readers to subject-specific vocabulary words, which are defined in the Words to Know section. Early readers may need assistance to read some words and to use the Table of Contents, Words to Know, Read More, Internet Sites, and Index/Word List sections of the book.

Table of Contents

fur

tail

ears

whiskers

legs

paw

4

Some cats live on farms.

Cats roam around farms.
Most farm cats live
outside and in barns.

tom

queen with kittens

8

A male cat is a tom.

A female cat is a queen.

Young cats are kittens.

Some farmers give food
and water to cats.

Cats help farmers
by catching mice and
other small animals.
Cats pounce on their prey.

Cats use their tongue to groom themselves.

16

Cats take many naps.

Cats purr.

Cats meow.

Words to Know

barn—a farm building where crops, animals, and equipment are kept

groom—to keep neat and clean; cats use their rough tongue to groom their fur.

meow—to make a noise like a cat; when a cat meows, it usually wants attention or is communicating with other cats.

pounce—to jump on something suddenly; cats have strong muscles that help them pounce quickly.

prey—an animal that is hunted by another animal for food; cats' prey includes rats, mice, birds, gophers, and frogs; some farmers feed cats very little food so that they will search for more prey.

purr—to make a low, soft sound

roam—to walk around without a certain place to go

Read More

Frost, Helen. *Cats.* All About Pets. Mankato, Minn.: Pebble Books, 2001.

Meadows, Graham. *Cats.* Animals Are Not Like Us. Milwaukee: Gareth Stevens, 1998.

Trumbauer, Lisa. *The Life Cycle of a Cat.* Life Cycles. Mankato, Minn.: Pebble Books, 2002.

Internet Sites

Track down many sites about cats.
Visit the FACT HOUND at *http://www.facthound.com*

IT IS EASY! IT IS FUN!

1) Go to *http://www.facthound.com*

2) Type in: 0736816607

3) Click on "FETCH IT" and FACT HOUND will find several links hand-picked by our editors.

Relax and let our pal FACT HOUND do the research for you!

Index/Word List

barns, 7
catching, 13
farmers, 11, 13
farms, 5, 7
female, 9
food, 11
give, 11
groom, 15
help, 13

kittens, 9
live, 5, 7
male, 9
meow, 21
mice, 13
naps, 17
outside, 7
pounce, 13
prey, 13
purr, 19

queen, 9
roam, 7
themselves, 15
tom, 9
tongue, 15
use, 15
water, 11
young, 9

Word Count: 71
Early-Intervention Level: 9

Credits
Heather Kindseth, series designer; Heidi Meyer and Patrick D. Dentinger, book designers; Deirdre Barton, photo researcher

Capstone Press/Gary Sundermeyer, cover, 4, 10, 16, 18, 20
Norvia Behling, 8 (top)
Unicorn Stock Photos/Eric Berndt, 1; Julie Haber, 8 (bottom); Aneal Vohra, 14
Visuals Unlimited/A.D. Copley, 6; Gary W. Carter, 12

The author dedicates this book to her friends Beth-Ann and B.R. O'Halloran and their cats, Touser, Babes, Black, and Grey.